Ballads of
BENGAL

Ballads of BENGAL

An Exploration Inside the Various Colors of Bengal

RAUNAK BARAL

PARTRIDGE

A Penguin Random House Company

To order additional copies of this book, contact
Partridge India
000 800 10062 62
orders.india@partridgepublishing.com

www.partridgepublishing.com/india

To Mumma and Babai, for being there always.

The danseuse

Spendthrift beauty,
On mostly undeserving
But such grace.
That the smallest of the small
Feel like kings.

Ghungroo rings when those feet
Touch the floor,
Tap, tap, tap
As she dances.
And a crowd mourns
The ending of a good performance.

Behind the mask,
Behind the facade
Lies just another woman,
In all her womanly ways.

A comb is important to her vanity,
Her saree, her dignity.
The sindoor that adorns her forehead,
A strong relic of her marriage.
Her Gita, the embodiment of purity.

She goes to the Ganga ghat everyday,
And offers flowers to the holy river.
Her face, like a pradeep in the
Great, black, shiny river water.

But when she dances,
She's a wily enchantress
An apsara of sorts.
Her kohl lined eyes,
The edge of reason.

Raining heavy

It's early morning,
And you wake up to find him gone.
No letters, no flowers
Just an empty bed.

Maybe he's gone out for something
And you make coffee for you both.
And you break your back to make breakfast
For you both.
But the entire morning passes,
And he's not back home.
You sit by the window
Waiting to see him at the door.
But he's not there...

You tenderly type a few teary messages
He doesn't reply.
The rain comes down like a memory recollected too often,
This bed will always lie empty you think,
As tears roll down your cheeks.
Nature drowns you in her best downpour,
The city lights are your friends,
They pass the message to each other,
As far as the city limits.
But he's nowhere to be found.

The big hollow buildings stand
Like mourners at a funeral,
You sing yourself a lullaby
And put yourself to sleep.
End the affair.
And your happiness for some time to come.

What hurts the most

When the skewed notes of evening jazz
Fail to permeate my soul.
I am thinking of you,
Soul incarnate,
My heart, really.

You think I'm a liar,
And that's okay,
Because what hurts the most
Is knowing that we both
Can never be together again.

What's wrong?
Why won't you talk to me?
Is it because I am in penance?
Do I deserve this?
Is it really too late to come back
And say "I love you"?

It's hard to deal with the pain
Of losing you,
Everywhere I go.
Baby you don't know,
I have changed over
And for the better...

Little after twelve

I waited for your telephone call
But the phone decided to be a snob,
I looked at the few LED blinks on the top,
It let me knew the phone was alive,
So was the environment.
And you were lost somewhere in the snaky alleys
Of my city.

It's a little after twelve,
And I wonder if you thought of me today,
The way I think of you.
Maybe you did,
I sit still and watch the rain outside.

I am coming out of my shell, I can feel it
Like a butterfly out of its coccoon,
I can see the light.
You wanted to see metamorphosis,
Didn't you?
And so you will see,
I have changed physically,
And in my mind, too,
But I still am the same person inside.
That didn't change.

My heart still flutters when it meets someone's eyes,
I still avoid their glances,
I am still shy,
I am still a tender-heart.
Maybe they wanted me to grow up,
What did they want exactly?
Iron, instead of soul?
I couldn't give them that.

I present to the world,
Beauty of mind,
If you can appreciate it.
And clear reason,
If you can understand it.

And as for my pain,
I have found someone.

Catharsis

Big wheels, on my shoulders
How I forgot to be a cog,
A small machine
In this universal mechanism.

As the surrounding cogs roll on my skin,
Which is not metal
Blood flows.
It falls to the ground,
And red-red roses grow.

The wheels run over my back and my head,
I'm ever running to meet their pace.
I see the light!
The machinery delivers me to it,
I am shone for a while,
With some societal grease.
And then I return to my everyday drudgery.
Always running,
Always running.

Like every slave,
I somehow love this nihilism.
The government sends me an email,
Asking me about my well being.
I tell them,
I'm not too well.
I'm sick,
I need water.
But there are no taps in my house.

No electricity,
So it's dark,
I'm sure there are no taps,
But they are telling me there are,
It's so dark I can't tell if there are.

What is the end to this?

Tumultuous love

Years after the original heartbreak,
I hear melody in my heart again
In the gardens and courtyards of my mind,
You are playing hide and seek with me,
And I think I see you.
Are you here for me?
You must be.

Because God tells me you were made for me,
I just hope, and hope, and hope
That you see it too.
If you do,
Then we'll play in that secret garden
And then it will be only us.
Under the maddening sky,
In this tumultuous love.

Time

I stood infront of the clock,
Like I stand,
Everyday since I was five.
When I learnt that when the big hand reaches 3,
Actually means fifteen in minutes.

Time ticks slowly by,
Pausing at every minute and second,
And for noone else.

When I waited for time to pass,
Time passed me by so quickly
That I couldnt grab it with my arms.
Now seven or eight years have passed by,
And I have lost a good four or five.
Elemental,
Yet rudimental for my progress.

I wonder if I stumbled or time did,
Or maybe we both did
On a fine summer's day.

I thought life is long,
And I whiled away the passing seconds
Doing absolutely nothing,
Refusing to be productive.

Then I found myself hanging from the hands
Of the clock itself.
Lying with arms and legs tied.
The clock struck twelve
And both needles pierced into my heart.

I heard the ominous ding-dong,
As a part of me died a soldier's death.
On a rugged empty battlefield.
Where I was the only fallen.

Musings of an idle mind

Yes, it's sad
Because I see you, melting away
Like frozen moisture on my window this morning,
I see you melting away into the long winding road,
Away from my home.

You are going into town,
To get us supplies for the week,
You even got a list,
Marmalade, beans and pork.
You do the shopping,
While I do the arranging.
I cook,
You stare,
Sipping on your wine glass.
With that record on,
Going on and on with hits from back in the day.

I wondered if my life went wrong,
Casually, because I could afford to think,
I wouldn't be, if something actually had.
But thinking about that gives me some reason to complain,
And I go on and on for hours about how
I am insufficient, and careless
You just smile,
I know you're getting irritated,
But I do that.
I'm testing you,
I want to see if you still love me like before,
You wouldn't scold me if you did.

I held my breath,
As I ranted on about inconsequential things
But you listened patiently,
Never opining.
Because, yes, that's the open trap
And I think you knew.
The moment you open your mouth,
You're either judging me,
Or you are too tired to carry on the conversation.
Both would work against you.

So I couldn't get you to open your mouth
You wily old man,
I know you are the very devil,
You read my mind don't you?

I should have run away with a sailor,
Or escaped to southern France
And married a French painter.
But here I am cooking for you,
Why?
Do you know that?

I'll tell you.

There are many reasons.

I adore you,
I am in awe of you.
I married you simply because you were
One of the brightest visionaries I have ever seen,
I love it when you talk.
Yes, I admit, you don't talk about politics,
Or war, or death,
But when you talk about God, or love, or beauty or nature
Everyone pays rapt attention, in the room.

And when you write,
Yes, when you write
You drown me in a sickness,
A dizzying, giddying sickness.
I am absorbed when you are reading out to me.
I think you are Sinbad,
And I am a mere Baghdadi.
And like him,
When you finish your story,
You offer me a smile, or a kiss, whichever
Like the gold coins that Sinbad used to distribute.
Well, old man, you don't have much money
But you do have a lot of affection.

When I say not a lot of money,
I don't mean to demean you,
I am happy with whatever you have given to me,
A few more odd years,
And we'll be getting that mercedes convertible.
And I'll ride it, while you sit with me.
Old man!
No smiling please,
You know I'm not a great driver.
I may bump it it a little.
But promise,
You won't get cross at me?

There,
That's like a good boy!
Wait?
Someone's at the door,
Oh, look who it is!
Mrs. Downey from the neighbourhood.
I'm sure she has some gossip about the neighbourhood.
I'll tend to her now.
And tell you what she told me over your evening cup of coffee,
I know how you love gossip, you letch!
Goodbye for now, my love.

Hold my hand

I reside in heaven,
Would you believe that?
I am watching you
From above a thoughtful cloud.

Virgin child,
I don't wanna die
Without knowing love first.
And this is one thing angels are scarce of;
I am lending you my hand
I don't have fairy potions
Or the looks,
Infact I have a very fat tummy.
And I want you to hold my hand.
I'll show you around,
My world.
My muses.
My idea of beauty.
And forever,
And eternity.

Lovers at March

If I fell in love
In a time, when it is condemned.
If I sang a song,
And I trusted,
In a dystopic world.
Would you bring down your sticks
On my back?
Just because I fell in love?

Words they're slipping out,
People come marching out,
I become the rotating statue
In the middle of anarchy.
People are pointing at me,
My blood becomes virtue.
On your hands,
On your face,
Let the red vermillion of victory
Paint the corners of our smiles.

I am the eternal child,
I dreamt of a world at peace.
Now there are demons in my world,
Poking knives at my heart.
Only the youth shall know,
And only the youth shall rise
Till tomorrow,
Till a brighter sunrise.

For bullets can break my body,
But they can't drown my voice.
One which has been risen,
In the kingdom of heaven.

The perpetrator's stick

We are only dreaming,
A few thousand hands are we.
Not as old as they'd like us to be.
Not really used to guns and sticks,
Not really used to punches and kicks,
Not used to have our clothes torn off.

We scream and we fight,
But the enemy always turns off the light
And in the darkness
They mutilate us.

I'm glad I don't watch the TV,
Not odd romanticism
But hatred for the 'purdah' system
Of our media.

I'm glad I never let anyone steal my spirit
For I forgot grudges and regrets
To go back to the same greens,
That cradled me for some two years.

I am glad, I am glad
That I was born in a time
When many visionaries existed,
And the statue of the king
Wasn't our greatest cultural heritage.

I expect to be a father someday,
And I hope my son or daughter lives
In a world free of torture or deceit,
But what have I?
Only words.
One brain.

And a back, which I dedicate to the revolution.
It's blood and muscle,
It will yield to the perpetrator's sticks.
But the bloody painting you leave behind,
Will be the memory of this September's revolution,
And the precursor of change.

Welcome to the gypsy band

Pour your sins in this
Earthen goblet.
Let us dance now,
You can leave your desire
For precious metals behind.
For, you have reached a place
Where these things do not exist.
Only love and harmony,
Only love and harmony.

The children play with flower wreaths,
On their heads.
The mothers are cooking,
Over unwarranted fires.
We are but a gypsy band you see.
If you want a drink and be jolly,
I'll pass you the bottle.

Let's sit by the fire,
And pass the peace pipe,
While the flamenco guitar plays.
The early morning sun rises,
And our festivities will have to end soon.
As we give our bodies some rest.
And then we will walk to the forest,
To hunt, and to bring back some firewood.

This is a spanish caravan, you see.
Maybe you want your fortune read?
That's Madam Isabella, famous card reader from the North,
Her ghost spirits tell her about the future.
Or, maybe we shall pass eh?
You too look a bit groggy.

The bloody University

Two boys,
Right after college met under a tree,
One in revolutionary panjabi pajamas,
One in torn cloak.
Weep no tears for his state,
He is a cursed one,
Only he is responsible for his state.
Because the moment the court was ready
To judge his case,
The world went on a vacation.
But the boy in the pajamas didn't care.

Together they went to the Maidan and drunk
Half a bottle of rum.
Drunk afterwards.
They decided to go to the Independent rally,
They danced their way to the front,
And delivered a combined speech
And the wet gunpowder in everyone's heart
Burnt up like flamethrowers.

Then they decided to go to the Cemetery,
Where many politicians were buried,
A couple of odd Basus, and Bhattacharyas and Guevaras.
They paid their respect and cried a few tears,
And sang jolly songs of his passage to heaven.
His?
Comandante's,
Whose else?

Next they went to the radio station,
Where they were making prank calls
And said unholy words to the Jack of hearts
Of a particular university,
Where outsiders are not allowed.
And the women there are 'dangerous juvenile delinquents'.

Then they came to the main gate of the university,
And parted ways,
One went into the future of the university.
And one quietly regressed in its past.

Raunak Baral

A laughable song

This is your life,
This is the moment
The limelight is upon you
And there are monsters waiting
In the backstage,
Waiting for you to fail.

Your dreams keep you awake at night.
Your peers don't really give a fuck,
And like minded people won't really have you
Because you didn't go to some wishy-washy university
And get a wishy-washy english degree.

Sometimes me and my guitar lament,
There seems to be noone who wants to listen
To a poor man's song.

Today everyone's rich,
Parents are pumping moolah
In fifteen year olds' pockets.
Noone gives a shit if she comes back home drunk.
Maybe she doesn't too.

Some odd black sheep in a flock of white,
How to keep them from going astray?
I think and ponder,
They have too many scars to heal.

No matter how much humanity strays away
From the word love,
No matter how much circumstances or struggles
Strengthen our hearts.
I will plant a flower of love,
Wherever Nature's teardrop fell on your scarred heart.
Healing it bit by bit.

Laugh at my sensibility,
But what if you find yourself
Stranded with nothing but your heart
A few years from now.
And noone to understand it?

Raunak Baral

My bold acquaintance

I see a sky of blue,
Because its autumn,
Folks are dancing to the Beatles,
Because the mood is so free
You can buy it at a grocer's
And pay nothing.

The sun is sparkling on the water,
Young lovers unite,
Old folks grumble,
God is not here yet.
Some memories need to be forgotten.

I am so biased,
About my happiness
That sad things don't cross my mind.
It's here forever that I will find myself.

The house is empty and I'm alone,
I am thinking of women and friendship
As I raise my glass.
One day we'll dance together,
When I find you.
One day we'll laugh in joy
At nothing at all.

Too much has been said about love and beauty,
Fairies can fly about my head all they want
They may even pour their magic potions,
I won't fall in love.
For in love I am lost,
I don't see night or day.
I want to walk the easy path,
Not indulging in love.
So God forgive me.

After winter comes,
And my hormones are raging
I will look into your eyes and I will say those words.
You will refuse me like every woman has.
I will leave a small memory in your mind,
Which you can remember when you're old.
And if I don't find love till then,
I will come and hold your hand.
Till then you can go on,
Not loving me.

You are dumb,
For love is such a sweet potion.
So intoxicating,
And so palpable.
A buried treasure,
A seaman's song.
A lover's plea,
Is it really that funny to neglect?

Too long

They parted,
Like cards,
On a weary sunset.
He had found other reasons to be happy,
And she never saw another face.

He wished she would not blame him,
But she couldn't help it,
She was hurt and cross.
The fate of their souls were written in pieces,
On freshly mined diamonds,
From Africa.
Or spread in the sea,
Where they moved with the currents
To find a land where they could live with each other again.

He seemed to stop rising,
Like the sun
Every morning
Only set at night.
She whispered sweet nothings in the ears of others.
And he would be hurt,
If he knew.
If he only knew.

Then she came a calling,
On an odd summer day,
He had fallen,
She was happy,
Karma, it was.
He understood why,
And gave her every opportunity to
Satisfy her vengeant whims,
Knowing she will never be the same again.
It was too long,
Even time had forgotten what she used to be like.

Raunak Baral

The nameless

So, you said
It would be a jiffy,
You'd just go around the bend
And come back.

I watched you leave,
And waited
For you to come back.
By now youve become a cartoon elephant
In my head.
I don't remember you anymore.

I'm drowning now,
In my own imagination.
I see a long hallway and I'm walking down.
If I stop at the right door I get to meet my favourite
Superheroes.
A little farther,
The Joker, is waiting for me
Wearing bandages,
Covered in blood,
Holding a knife.

I don't want to go back,
I just want to find safety.
A great scorpion is at my back,
In a well full of scorpions,
That is how I came here.
Don't want to go back.

I murmur your name.
I don't know if you shall show me the way.

The Old England Gentleman's Club

You walk through the archaic gates,
Carefully adorned with leaves,
You leave your conscience behind.
And enter "The Old England Gentleman's Club".

There is every vice on offer,
Hung naked from a chandelier
In the middle.
Glowing bright as a virtue,
And people danced.

With women in various stages of undress,
And men fawning on them.
It's a regular sight from sunrise to sunset.

Beer spills on expensive cloaks,
But noone really cares,
The breathlessness of passion
Keeps their heads busy
And faces turned away from poignancy.

A rueful tune plays on the sad piano,
There are no two lovers around
Just a group of people exploiting love's love
In the name of lust.

Lustful sinews,
In the human maze of macaroni it seemed.

With oysters on his feet,
He walked tumbling in,
Measured his luck in ounces,
And drank it from the peg.

Quite drunk he bumped into a semi naked
Maid.
She held his face to her bosom,
But he was seeking other mother's honey
Not interested in human offerings.

He went to the card room,
Smoky and indistinct,
His lean bent frame,
His shiny hair and electric eyes
Betrayed every inch of a gambler.

He took a few more drinks,
And engrossed in the play
He made a couple of people lose
A lot of money.
Better's instinct,
I would say.

When he got up from the table,
He was a couple of hundreds richer.
And then he could afford the luxuries of the house.
He jumped like a hungry dog on the women.

By the morning,
When the cinder was all that was left
And smoke was running up the chimney,
They all exited bottle in their hands.
On the grimy outside street,
Drunk in life,
And promiscuity.

Azalea

You, an ailurophile
Me. A masochist.
We were both in love,
But with different things.
I loved my hurt,
And you loved feline creatures.

Believe me when I say so,
Love doesn't come ordinarily,
You had cat eyes,
So, your vision automatically allowed you to
Fall in love with your cats.
Sharing body parts much.

I had eyes that could see my cracked heart,
Which didn't brew the magic potion of love anymore
I saw my soul,
Big, black, hollow and empty.
I am used to living like this,
In the celebration of my pain,
For it is in this pain,
I can feel something human.

I touched your skin,
No currents ran down my body,
But my breath stopped,
I don't know why.
I didn't feel love.
Just a moment's insecurity.

Your touch, so magic and so fluid
Only makes me want to die,
As I would rather have a memory of you
In my afterlife
Than a lifetime of pleasure.
With you.
You came.
But too late.

Magnolia

It is here,
And here alone
That men and women
Have sacrificed their hearts
On tall sticks of the pall-bearer.

When one heart slowly infuses into another,
Which one poisons the other?
Which one renders love black?
What is the end?
Even when the end is decided.

We stall the end till as far as we can,
Sometimes almost till the next life.
But the end is inevitable,
As much as the frivolities of life
And the constancy of death.

It is in this death,
That passion breeds dominance,
And jealousy, hate and envy.

The glass of spirit,
When raised to the lips
Releases ghosts of women,
Who used to surround me.
They talk to me.
They promise me they are mine,
But I can never call them by their names
Or see their faces,
Or feel their bodies.

Come as a flower,
And floating in the ether
Unmindful as a child dancing,
She looks to me,
As if she will find the ends to this passion
Tonight,
In my arms.
She looks to me,
And speaks out of her eyes,
Lustful advances
Which she otherwise could not have said.
She is standing,
The invitation is clear.
My spirit leaves the body,
And joins her.
The lonely body lies lifeless,
As we slowly dance under the stars.

A bolt out of the blue

It's a shy night,
The moon is wearing silver
And the sky is blushing red.
I am riding my car
Over to Veronica's place.
We shall drink coffee,
And then a spot of wine.

Before leaving,
My wife asked me
"Are you going to eat outside?"
And I said,
"I'll be bringing candles and champagne"
And I winked.
She laughed, her usual free laughter.
And I chuckled out of sight.

"So...", Veronica said,
"Am I looking good?"
"Like a siren...", I said.
She looked satisfied.
And she pored over me
With the things she cooked for me.
For your information,
Veronica is my sister.

It's a sly night,
The wind is quite tricky,
We are standing in the verandah
In the cold winter wind,
Watching the stars.
And smiling between ourselves.

She asked me about my wife,
I said she's fine
As long as she doesn't try to eat her diet.
Because then she goes overboard,
And bores me,
With the drab boiled vegetables,
Which are really not to my taste.

She discusses the state of affairs,
And I nod my head with a smile on my face.
Only if she could find a worthy man.
"Veronica", I say,
"Find someone before you grow fat and old."
She makes a face.
"You do know men like young women"
"So it is, Raunak. But I hardly look a day older than 30."
"So may it be."
And I winked.
She wound up her face.
I laughed.
And patted her on the back.

I promise to her next time I am over,
I will bring one of my exciting male friends,
Who are under 30.
And she glows.
My eyes ache to see such perfection.
We finish the wine.
And I leave.

I meet the doctor on the way,
He calls out to me,
"Baral!"
"Congratulations man!", he said
"What for?", I do not understand.
"For making your wife pregnant!"
"Oh....yes...that!"
Damn I couldn't pretend I don't know.
"You don't know?"
"Now I do"
"Haha. Bugger off home now. She shouldn't be staying up late"
"A cognac off you next time!"
"Absolutely!"

It's late,
But I make my way to the market.
I buy a few orchids,
And a card that said,
"Thank you..."
And nothing else.
And I make way home.

She, I can see, is waiting up for me,
I knock the door...

Raunak Baral

They gifted me salvation

And on the day,
They decided to forgive me
They stripped my pride naked
And exposed all my evil deeds,
Some of them were embarassing and private
And I felt layer after layer of my clothing disappearing,
As they furiously tugged.
Salvation, I knew
Was waiting for me
After they mentioned all my nefarious acts in public.

I at that time,
Was exposed to Buddhism
Born a Hindu.
I sensed a Hindu crowd standing,
With eyes wide open
Comparing my travesty to the disgarmentation of Draupadi.

The two were different things,
My kin, the Hindus thought it was wrong
That prayers and rituals could solve my woes
But the Buddhist wisdom demanded that I pay the price
For my own Karma.

And at the end of it,
When I was completely derobed.
Everyone I ever hurt forgave me.
My pride floated in the pits of hell like a dead eagle,
And my inner bodhisattva raised his head.

The Buddhist monks were singing songs of bravery and courage,
And a long way to go.
I have just reached salvation.

Fleeting love

She won't fall in love, no
Her ties that bind lie in someone else's heart.
It's so hard to convince her to
Talk.

She finds her freedom in the sun
And the breeze,
That blows.
She travels with the gypsies,
In spanish caravans.
Her kneelength skirt sometimes revealing fair skin.

She is an enigma to me,
A maze not entered.
The atrocity of love,
The punishment that it is
And the tasks that it demands,
Is making me weak my Lord.

Make me a dozen times charming,
And maybe I will hold her gaze for longer.
And see her raven smile more often.

Raunak Baral

One bold woman

The way that lace hangs from your body,
The way you are sipping on that wine,
I got lost looking at your wet eyes,
You dance for me.

You come over me,
You dance for me,
You strip for me.
You're at ease with me.
That's because,
You're mine.

I take you by the hair,
And make you understand
The pain of the longing I felt for so long
And we were bound at the hip.

You moan,
But I smother you with my kisses
So you just breathe heavy.

We do away with society's no-nos
And splurge on a relationship that's a taboo.
If you were reading this,
Then you'd know,
The degree of lust
I feel for you.

Going somewhere nice

Take me somewhere nice,
Driving in your car,
Through long empty roads,
With the moon for company.
And the darkness,
With a sense of foreboding,
It hasn't been too long
Since we got the license to roam nights.
What if a call comes from home?
Where shall you tell them you are?

Feeling the night breeze on your face,
You become thoughtful,
That expression on your face
Betrays sadness.

I play the car stereo,
Something soft and nice.
You know I'm just trying to lift your mood,
You smile a wry smile.
I want to say 'Jahnavi,'
'There's hope for us',
'We aren't the only two beings on this planet',
'With alcohol as our enemy'.

You catch me staring at you,
'Huh?', you say.
If I told you Jahnavi,
You would start doubting yourself again,
And then we will go back into the loop.
I'd rather stay silent,
And wait for you to say something.

We go to the meetings,
And you were so excited to be going back.
Do you realise Jahnavi,
We are like mercury,
We cannot stand on our own,
One bad word, And we come crashing down.
Our darkness is our enemy,
It consumes us.
We cannot come out from it,
Unless, unless,
We give it a shot.

'Happy Birthday Jahnavi',
Your one year clean.
And you look at me and say,
'Next year we celebrate yours'...

The friend who never left

They floated out of memories,
And started dancing infront of me.
These few friends I had in the past,
And those who do not speak with me anymore.
We had some lovely time as children,
And as young adults.

I remember once,
On a trip to Mumbai,
We blew almost all our money on the
Air tickets for me.
And then the rest on the expensive food,
In Bandra.

I still remember that you came to get me,
At the airport.
Before that,
In the airline bus,
At Mumbai,
We ventured through,
And there was a small lane,
I stared into the darkness,
Which was dimly lit by a few streetlamps,
And there were a couple of cars.
I was breathing heavily,
Didn't know what to expect.
How you would look,
How the city had changed you,
For I hadn't seen you in two months.
And Delhi had changed me plenty,
New hairstyle and all,
Complete with an eyebrow piercing.

Then I saw you at the gate,
You were waiting with that smile on your face,
Your hair in a braid,
I felt like I was in heaven,
Really!
When I held your hand.
I was still doubting myself,
And I gained my composure,
Telling myself it's stupid!
This relationship!
You, me...
And God.

I stayed silent,
You kept asking me how you looked,
I said 'nice', as if I didn't mean it.
You were used to getting hurt by me,
So you didn't think twice.

We had that expensive dinner,
You said you had eaten,
But I really doubted that.
You had a bit from me,
Because I wouldn't let it be.

We sat on the rocks in Bandra,
We went to the pretentious Cafe Coffee Day,
In Carter road.
What I really wanted,
Was to make love to you,
And we tried,
On the rocks,
Our very own sex on the beach.

Two years hence,
I saw you crying,
When I told you I'm leaving for rehab,
You got me a card.
I don't remember what was written.
But there was a storm going on within me.

Now today,
You're not there,
But you've left traces of you
All over my life.
Not a day passes when I don't think of you,
The memories speak to me,
And I am talking to you again like we used to,
You never grow old in my mind.
You tell me how things should be done,
And sometimes you tease me
By staying quiet.
Are you hurt?

Today,
I miss you,
Because all the while that you were there,
I never realised the value of you.

Raunak Baral

The Inferno speaks

I am an amorphous solid. I lack shape and form. I am made up of lava. I exist in *'dark'*. I am fire. I am warm, hot, blistering. I devour men and animals. I am Inferno.

I explode like a volcano, subside like a lover's embrace. I am alive. I am the *'punisher'*. Red fangs of vengeance burn in my body. And I feel sacrilege as I dig my blistering teeth into innocent men's bloodstreams. I suck out blood. I punish them for *'being'*. For existing, and committing mistakes. Things that I feel is wrong.

I am fiery amoeba. I wrap myself around the earth.

I am a dreamer, please tell me I'm a *human being*. I want to cry, I want to love. But all I can feel is continuous combustion and explosion. My liquid heart explodes lava and gets stuck in time-space.

I want to devour no more. I want to be a French painter painting the Pyrenees. I want to be a Norwegian fisherman. I want to be a German. I want to drink beer.

I want to have parents, I want to grow up, I want to be a kid, I want to *die*.

I want to feel rain in spain, I want to see teardrops of heaven drip along my umbrella. I want to light fire, and muse about ancient man and discovery of fire.

These are tales the men tell me. These are things they have experienced. I hear, and breathe a sigh of fire and smoke. My heart strains to leave.

I ask God for forgiveness. Why was I made such? Why can't I experience beauty? Why can't I love? What is the meaning of my existence? Am I just a tool? I want to be limbs of the society like these men. They fable me in their lores, they detest me, they abhor me. Why can't I be *loved*?

Monsoon

Monsoon is almost gone,
The sky roars passionately still
What we'll be missing is the mangoes
The rainwater filled fuchkas,
And long wet walks.

Like an artist on an empty canvas,
Lightning streaks down
And subtle ragas play in my room,
I sit by the window and wonder
Will the rains flood the street infront of my house?
Then it's a holiday,
More rain watching on a lonely day.

The shadows glow in their dark hue,
They passionately hug the furniture
As the flute plays on to ecstacy.
Next stop: another astral plane.

Raunak Baral

Crying in the rain

I am the little boy,
Who is standing by the door
Hiding his face,
While all of you
Decide my fate.
There's anger
And curious expressions on your faces.
Shouting at each other,
Wanting to be heard.
While I'm crying my heart out,
My tears they disappear like a wary fly
Like raindrops on a glass window.
I can't pretend anymore,
I don't like you,
I can't live like this anymore.
This time maybe,
Just maybe,
You're not going to throw me
Into a hellhole.
You're going to treat me like a human being
You're going to give me the choice
To be my own master.
You are going to overlook your ego,
And you are not going to fight me anymore.
For I am weaponless,
And your swords and knives,
They hurt.

Raining heavy

It's early morning,
And you wake up to find him gone.
No letters, no flowers
Just an empty bed.

Maybe he's gone out for something
And you make coffee for you both.
And you break your back to make breakfast
For you both.
But the entire morning passes,
And he's not back home.
You sit by the window
Waiting to see him at the door.
But he's not there...

You tenderly type a few teary messages
He doesn't reply.
The rain comes down like a memory recollected too often,
This bed will always lie empty you think,
As tears roll down your cheeks.
Nature drowns you in her best downpour,
The city lights are your friends,
They pass the message to each other,
As far as the city limits.
But he's nowhere to be found.

The big hollow buildings stand
Like mourners at a funeral,
You sing yourself a lullaby
And put yourself to sleep.
End the affair.
And your happiness for some time to come.

Raunak Baral

The danseuse

Spendthrift beauty,
On mostly undeserving
But such grace.
That the smallest of the small
Feel like kings.

Ghungroo rings when those feet
Touch the floor,
Tap, tap, tap
As she dances.
And a crowd mourns
The ending of a good performance.

Behind the mask,
Behind the facade
Lies just another woman,
In all her womanly ways.

A comb is important to her vanity,
Her saree, her dignity.
The sindoor that adorns her forehead,
A strong relic of her marriage.
Her Gita, the embodiment of purity.

She goes to the Ganga ghat everyday,
And offers flowers to the holy river.
Her face, like a pradeep in the
Great, black, shiny river water.

But when she dances,
She's a wily enchantress
An apsara of sorts.
Her kohl lined eyes,
The edge of reason.

What hurts the most

When the skewed notes of evening jazz
Fail to permeate my soul.
I am thinking of you,
Soul incarnate,
My heart, really.

You think I'm a liar,
And that's okay,
Because what hurts the most
Is knowing that we both
Can never be together again.

What's wrong?
Why won't you talk to me?
Is it because I am in penance?
Do I deserve this?
Is it really too late to come back
And say "I love you"?

It's hard to deal with the pain
Of losing you,
Everywhere I go.
Baby you don't know,
I have changed over
And for the better...

Raunak Baral

Little after twelve

I waited for your telephone call
But the phone decided to be a snob,
I looked at the few LED blinks on the top,
It let me knew the phone was alive,
So was the environment.
And you were lost somewhere in the snaky alleys
Of my city.

It's a little after twelve,
And I wonder if you thought of me today,
The way I think of you.
Maybe you did,
I sit still and watch the rain outside.

I am coming out of my shell, I can feel it
Like a butterfly out of its coccoon,
I can see the light.
You wanted to see metamorphosis,
Didn't you?
And so you will see,
I have changed physically,
And in my mind, too,
But I still am the same person inside.
That didn't change.

My heart still flutters when it meets someone's eyes,
I still avoid their glances,
I am still shy,
I am still a tender-heart.
Maybe they wanted me to grow up,
What did they want exactly?
Iron, instead of soul?
I couldn't give them that.
I present to the world,
Beauty of mind,
If you can appreciate it.
And clear reason,
If you can understand it.

And as for my pain,
I have found someone.

Candice

Clinging to his arms,
She breathed out, in pleasure.
He looked at their union in the mirror,
Strange symmetry,
How everything fits.

The music playing in the background
Reaches a crescendo,
She rides him,
And feels the rush inside her.
She bites his shoulder,
Just to feel if its real.
Like a whale surfacing,
Something just made its way out of her heart,
Welling in her heart,
And made it swell with emotions.
There was no going back, in love.
She imagined them sitting on a bench
In a stretch of greens,
She thought of forever
And always.

She thought,
"I guess that's love,
I can't pretend otherwise anymore".

Evening.
She lies in her room,
Cigarette butts in the ashtray.
She's crying,
The phone beneath her bosom.
Spiders crawl out of her mouth,
Spiders of insanity,
Spiders of hurt and heartbreak.
She's tied to this human frame.
What will cause her release?
Her, and lovers like her.

Raunak Baral

Adventurer in an armchair

Tom Adler is a real gentleman,
Every morning he wakes up to
A cup of tea, hot eggs and bacon,
Breakfast in bed, that too!

Then he gets dressed in
A dapper black suit,
Picks up his walking stick,
And struts his way to the market.
"Hello, Mrs. Magpie, what a wonderful day!"
And he comes across small children
Playing ball on the streets,
Lovingly he messes their hair.
Then,
"Ah! Mr. Brown, when are you coming down?
We still have that unfinished game of chess, y'know..."

Then he picks up a brown bag,
And fills it with the greenest cucumbers,
The reddest apples,
And some beans.

Then he makes his way to the pier,
He's got a seat reserved for him there.
He gets a cup of coffee,
And sinks in his chair.
He sees the seagulls floating in the air,
And sometimes swooping down to catch their prey.
And he thinks of distant lands,
The great wall of China,
And Chinamen wearing rice hats.
He thinks of the great kingdom of Spain,
And men playing spanish guitars sitting next to fires
Carelessly, in beaches.
He thinks of Africa,
The virgin forests, the great Sahara
The lions and the spiders.
And he thinks,
"What a pity,
The mind doesn't travel as fast as the heart does.
Dreams be dreams."

Raunak Baral

Dear you

I'm looking for the sun,
Dear friend, can you take me away from the rain?
Soothe my tears,
And take away my pain?

You're thinking of me,
And I'm thinking of you
In the same old way.
The only difference is
We're not the same.

I'll light a candle,
If it brings you near
I'll try to bring you
In by the year.
You know I love you,
Not as I have loved before
But more and more and more.

Penance, Coffee and Stardust.

Penance, Coffee and Stardust
In a strange cafe,
In a mad neighbourhood.
Tapping my feet to the tune of
Spanish guitars,
Cabotage.

Mad love, bleeding red
Exploding in the air sometimes,
Floating like a pixie in a meadow
Consumes me.
She looks at me slowly sipping on her coffee.
Her eyes filled with the curious mysticism
That almost dares ask a question,
Or is bothered with the world,
Dispassionately indifferent.
Velas, Velas, Velas mi amor.

Your black eyes and your black hair
Casually dispassionate,
Your wrist below your chin
And your platinum bangle
Conveyed a sense of Bourgeoisie calm.

Raunak Baral

We took a walk down by the river
Your arm locked in mine
We watched the boats from the bridge,
How calm the scenery seemed.
Paradise painted in the pink of the setting sun
And the vengeful river dark and serene.

You said no words,
But as you stood there in the wind
My mind captured an image of you
Zephyr.
Penance, coffee and stardust.

Hatred

This is it!
My loquacious friend,
This is it! We have found it!
Paradise, Shangri-La whatever you call it.
This is where the world begins and ends.
He twisted his naked torso and bade his friend follow him,
Two microscopic males, they lit a sacrificial fire
Near a female vagina.
They watched the genital rise and fall, in ecstacy
Which the fire was putting it to.

Inside a woman moaned,
Lost in the wilderness of Kama-Sutra, manifested by only herself.
She doesn't need a partner,
Neither male nor female.
She is the sun, she is the moon, the night and day
All by herself,
She makes love to herself.
"This is the being, this is the creature!", He shouted.
"She can exist without company!"

Her female genital was the source of human Nirvana,
Peace derived from one's own self, and a plethora of lip-biting ecstacy.
However, it is viewed as a tool, for someone else's gratification,
And yet in itself, quite as useless and cold as a rock.
But is not so.
It is the gateway to heaven, mother of creation
Lip-biting ecstacy I say.

So, boots came in the door of the small hut
The two microscopic cherubs took shelter behind the hill of pleasure,
Above the genital.
The man dropped his gun on the floor.
And the cold sunlight, almost nonchalant flooded the soft body of his wife.
Beer was dripping from his lips, which was covered in a salt and pepper beard.
He felt no lust,
Just disgust.
"Woman!", he exclaimed.

The woman went on with her object,
Of satisfying herself, no shame spared.
For in the course of time,
The divine Lily of her sexuality had turned into the fierce hermaphrodite Hibiscus.
She was receptor and conqueror both.
Woman had turned into superbeing!

The absence of sexuality between the two creatures bound in lust,
Mistakenly identified as 'Love' for centuries, was striking.
Love is a mechanism of hydraulic pumping of hormones in the human body,
You see her eyes you feel a rush,
That is just blood rushing into your stomach,
A primal instinct.
One which says, it's okay to move to bed.

The cherubs rushed out,
And they had hellish excitement in their eyes
"The supernova!", they chanted and exhaled.
The woman came in a burst,
And wet the cloth she was sleeping on.
The man unable to control his disgust,
Got up, his boots kissing the floor beneath them in a tight noisy smooch,
And slapped the woman, firm across the face.
Anger filled her eyes.
Her half-done orgasm, withdrew itself back into her body.
Hatred,
That's what we live with.

Raunak Baral

You don't need to bother

They don't think twice,
Before they blame me, they indict me
No they don't need to bother,
They don't need to see whether I'm breathing.

You need to build me a memorial,
Upon which you will lay my body
As I lie dying,
And light that fire,
One that will purge my sins.
No, they don't need to bother.

You don't need to sing hymns,
At my funeral.
There shall be no tears,
For I know I shall not be taking with me
Any human emotions.

No songs, no laments
You don't need to bother,
I don't need to live.
Just remember me as a delinquent
Who strived hard to be remembered.

They with their invisible knives
Scarred my soul, my body, my spirit
I can't feel anything now!
No, you don't need to bother,
You don't need to care.

An ordinary woman

She left her blue jeans,
Her tank top,
And her funky jewelry back at her parents' house.
She walked with a wobbly knee,
She bowed her head,
And cried,
Her last tear as an unwedded 'wife'.

Isn't that all they are meant to be?
Some man's wife.

She crossed the holy fire,
And entered into the kingdom
Of her husband.
She sacrificed some of her dreams,
And broke millions of hearts,
Of those who were waiting for her.

Who is she?
She is a woman.
She is God's second best creation.
She is a mother.
She is a daughter.
Maybe a sister.
She has so many roles to play,
Yet one body.
How can one sacrificial fire bind her soul
To her husband's clothing?
She follows him in his fray?

Maybe she loved another man?
Maybe he wasn't 'good enough'
For her parents?
I am twenty five and I don't know what money can buy,
But money can definitely buy you a piece of ass.

Nishabd

When this vacant mind
Remembers you,
I am filled with such a love
That only heaven finds.

You are playing amongst trees
In my mind,
And I have seen your face.
But I do not want to call you mine,
Lest it scratch your freedom.
For a bird is most beautiful,
When it is flying amongst the pink clouds
With nothing to block its feathers.

Maharani, this love song is a homage to you
I smile as you try to be graceful,
I want to hold you by the waist
As you miss a step
Or when you trip a little on your long dress.
But you don't know,
I only smille.

You try to be witty,
In this *majlish*,
You have admirers of your wit.
But, none of your tenderness
As you peep from the door.
And the *pidim* burns bright
As I stare into your doe like eyes
You stay the night,
And we ask each other questions
Written in ink on *Chinar* leaves.
You ask me why?
I ask you how.

And the night rolls on.
To dawn...

Naxalite

I am born in Naxalbari,
I am born of hatred, I am born of exploitation
I am adivasi, I am Santhal
I am the raging fire burning in the forests.

I am dead, I am alive
I burn in the heart of the Naxalite.
I was raped, murdered, pillaged.
I went to bed without anything to eat,
My baby is dying of malnutrition
My husband is a chronic alcoholic
And beats me up at night.

This is a gun,
This is what I will raise against them.
They tell us about Mao-Tse-Tung,
They teach us alphabets and political ideology,
They tell us to fight for ourselves.
They teach us to sacrifice our blood
For the upliftment of our kind.

That man is police,
That man is a politician,
That man rapes us, he kills us
So I will eat his soul,
And damn it to hell.
If hell existed.
For people like us, they tell us
The concept of heaven and hell is too rich.

A house of cards

I carry a weight everyday,
Of being an acceptable member of society.
I build my house
Like an ant builds a house of cards.
Happiness lasts for only so long.

These doors took more than wood to build,
These doors that keep us safe
From the hyenas that roam outside.
These doors that separate us
From the cold of the streets,
And the rains and the sun.

I am carrying a legacy,
Of protecting my near and dear.
I'm playing with my wicker bow and arrows.
Then suddenly God shines down his light,
And asks me to follow.

I am afraid,
What if it takes me away from
These faces I love.
I would like nothing better than
To serve them all my life,
Sitting right here in my 'home'.

But useless am I,
A pound of flesh and muscles.
What use am I if I'm not bringing
Money to the home?

That is exactly what keeps me from straying,
Whenever I'm doing too much for myself
My heart starts palpitating,
"Come back, duty calls..."
I say to myself.
For I would be ashamed to call myself a man,
If,
My aging parents are lying alone at home
Waiting for me to return,
With the dinner spread out at the table,
Giving each other nervous glances,
For I haven't called in two or three hours.

God knows I have given them enough reason
To be scared,
I'm not brave enough anymore to say
"Screw the world, I can take care of myself"
My fears revolve around my parents' peace.
Are they at peace?
Have they slept soundly at night?

God, you had to play with my life
You could have kept it just at that,
I don't mind, really, anymore
Being thrown into hellish places behind lock and key.
I don't mind losing my head anymore,
And I'm not afraid of those insane people on the roads
That I keep seeing,
I won't turn into one of them.
For, in the last seven years if you had done anything good to me
It is that you made me a fighter,
A fighter that will fight tooth and nail for his survival.
You threw me in the pits.
It was a long way out.
A very long way.

Raunak Baral

But I hold nothing against you, God
It's your daily amusement,
I'm your favourite enemy
A rather 'powerless' enemy,
Stranded on a desert island.

No I won't sell my soul
To get rid of my misery,
I will fight this fight
And I know it isn't against you.
It's quite funny actually,
You trip me and make me fall
The next moment you're holding my hand
Picking me up from the pit I fell in.

You're a strange one oh Lord,
You tell me what I am doing wrong,
But you won't tell me what I'm looking for.

Jesus never came

Another afterglow,
Another lonely highway
Another bottle of Vodka.
Another night wasted,
Because Jesus didn't come.

She holds the cross tight in her hand,
Yes she's a drunk,
She's not too proud to say.
She keeps chanting,
"I'm lost without you".

And she was,
Lost without him
How was she supposed to be strong without him?
He who had been all her life?

He said sweet words of forever,
Then disappeared just without a trace.
She waited for him, embracing the booze.
Now she has wrinkles around her eyes.

No she is not,
Taking too good a care of herself.
Her room's a mess.
The miles just keep rolling,
As she drives on.

She needs love, Someone's touch
Someone to say 'always' is true.
Maybe he is pining at the other end of the world.
Who knows?
Jesus never came.

Fragile

So summer's gone,
Yet the rains remain.
You still rested in my fragile heart,
Which you broke maybe two or three times.
But I like a scavenger picked up the pieces,
And glued them together.
Now it looks like a himalayan kid,
With teeth splaying out at odd angles.

Let's gather round and thank our stars,
For us being as fragile as we are.
We give away our hearts to people who don't need them,
It's like gifting a chocolate to a kid who has too many.
He'll probably throw it away.
Not knowing the value of it.

And how many times have i told you
I love you, and in oh-so-many ways,
My love I lay like a blanket over the stars,
So that when you raise your eyes to look at the night sky,
You may feel my still, yet hidden, presence in your life.

Something in my mind says,
You are my Karma,
Which I have to expiate.
You keep reminding me how fragile I am everyday,
And I thank you for that.
I am no superman.
I never pretended to be.

On and on we choose to move on,
On our own separate paths.
But I can see you from mine.
This love was never meant to be.
You are too different from me.
I am not the man of your fancies.

Woman (Part one)

Looks like a sad day at work?
Temptress?
The man of the moment,
Is not sharing a glass with you
After a polo match anymore.
Sad truth is,
He's getting married.
To someone who he has deemed
More beautiful than you,
Kinder than you,
And definitely a better life partner.

Oh, probably you were never on the list.
That sneer seems to say,
Let her spend a day with him,
He'll find she's awful
Or she'll run gutless.
How can that bitch handle that stud?
Mercy, oh me!
You trip on the waiter carrying the drinks,
It spoils your sari.
You spit venom at him.
And he keeps his head bent,
As he utters apologies.

Time to go home.
You undress at your apartment in posh Bandra,
And wear a negligee, with your high black heels.
"I hope he's coming tonight"
You smile as you think of your casual lover,
One of the desparate ones you would drop
As casually you would drop your hanky.

And the evening rolls by.
And he doesn't call.
So she thinks,
Let's call Mother.
You chat for an hour or two.
About the 'pretentious' bride.
And how ugly everyone from the bride's family was.
Mom says,
"I never understood why you fancied him at all!"
"Really?"
"He was never our class. New money I say".

You turn on the TV to watch your favourite show,
You gaze like a zombie on the screen,
And eat your popcorn
And your icecream.

Devil temptress,
You look like angel of mercy.

Raunak Baral

Double trouble(You know you meant it)

It wasn't long back till the sky broke,
And thunder fell,
In your life.
Shattering that glasshouse of your dreams.
A hard price to pay for your sins.

You built that house back,
Bit by bit,
And now cynics throw stones at your palace.

You spend all your day infront of the computer,
The monster in your environment
Devours your senses.

Till one day, you found the light,
You found yourself,
Lurking dangerously close to a cliff.
And then mother calls,
She calls you back into society.

You now stand infront of windows sometimes,
And breathe muted expressions,
Sometimes you wonder, how beautiful
Is the environment surrounding you.

The clouds and the greens,
And everything in betweenl
You are an ordinary person now,
With an extraordinary dream.

Love note

Tú eres la joya de mi ojos senorita,
I've seen your eyes in the dim light of the dying sun, bleeding red
I have seen your eyes in the shadows that evening force into the world,
I have seen your eyes in the early sun,
And I have found mirth, happiness, and longing.

Do you dare eat from the forbidden fruit?
For I like the pitiful devil am offering this to you,
Bite right out of my Adam's apple,
It is yours, vampire.

You have seen fire,
But I have seen more,
For when the flamenco plays
And the hearts rush to meet grace,
I hereby gift my heart to you.

Velas, velas, velas, mi amor.

Murder

See, see yourself,
Here we are sitting in a room,
And I have not spoken about you any more than anyone else in the room.

Of late I have taken to more dangerous things,
Murder...
Murder of the soul,
Murder of the mind.
For I shall murder someone who is close to me,
I will bring his heart out,
And I will scream
"Do you forgive me? You fallen! Do you forgive me?"
And we shall meet eye to eye,
And you shall lament your life.
And I shall breathe into you,
The gift of reincarnation.

Land Ahoy!

I'm running, I'm running in a field
It's full of air, clean oxygen
I want to get free,
I want to live it all.
Get liberated.
Come fuck me with your thoughts,
Tell me your dreams,
Let's live each night,
Like there's no tomorrow.
In the day we'll go to the forest and dance,
In the evening, we shall light a fire and play flamenco on the guitar,
And we will dance to spanish tunes.
We will free our minds.

I am king, king of a nomad's land,
Where we live free,
Like men and women, freed from society's ties.
Let's go beyond countries and religions,
Let's just live as one.

Raunak Baral

Men

O' great giver,
We are not playing hunger games anymore.
We are soldiers,
Do or die.
Brave sons of the mother's soul,
Who won't slow down in the face of death or infamy.

SHOW US YOUR GUNS!
Such was the shout,
Flames engulfed them,
They withstood all pain.
The game has been played,
We are all men now.

The silhouette that speaks...

Did you chant Nam-Myoho-Renge-Kyo?
And I was happy, my friend was back.
He was speaking through music, mystic and absence of light.
I held my cigarette and drew a puff and smiled,
I just saw my face looking back at me
Looking a little shaggy with small strands of beard jutting out.
Afternoon glory?

Redeemer

Light thy fire,
Let us run tonight
Towards thy funeral pyre.
We shall light thee
In mirth and mercy,
Thou shall be forgiven of all sins
Absolved.

Not until,
Not until haha,
Thou hast offended me.
Then I face thee at a deep black lake,
In the city of the dead,
The dark eye of the Hamunaptra,
Raising and punishing your soul.
Thou shalt know it as the lake of fire,
And me as your redeemer.

Out of Ra's arm I escape
Purer than a single ray of light,
I am the redeemer,
Sayest my name.

And finally when your soul is broke,
I shall give thee a chance to live again
Live like a human,
Offering the Lord, a gift, that of thy soul
And Time shall dance its slow dance of death
Thou shall disperse
And meet me again at life.

If thou chance to kill me,
Fear not for I shall return
Exalted and bloodthirsty
I shall hold your entrails high up in the sky,
And feed them to the dogs of doom.

For I am absolved,
Purer than sunlight
Your redeemer.

Raunak Baral

Abstraction

You play the lyre my friend,
Because I am listening to my soul
Old backstabbing piece of jesus christ memorabilia.

You dance the disco beat my friend
Because my girl she danced the coco-jambo
Among the pines.
'Dotted with firs.'
Her wrist was,
She wears a velvet glove.

You bring the demonstealer
Because I have set a soul free
It's on fire
Cafe Nirvana.

Yeah, maybe, why not, sexy!
You don't know till you drop your pants.

Boom Bass, shoot the fish
I be a crazy munchin on wafers,
Potshot, mugshot, sirens on spree
Yeah Yeah, lore of the Lord.
Thou set us free.
Midnight song.
Avicadish.

This is for you my love,
Summer clothing is "Aw so sexy..."
But you will never know how it feels to love me,
Brandish your weapon
Yeah Yeah, I set you free
In a song.
Avicadish.

Mothers and sisters

Massacre, murder, maderization
Fifty beautiful niggers in bloom
Kurt Cobain drowning in blue ocean,
Beautiful baby I can see your face
In a sunflower.

I chose murder, I chose murder my friend
Of you, Of humankind
Your love, your hate
You thought they were just words?
After the last time...that left you numb?

Maybe he is drunk
Maybe he doesn't care,
But he's your Dad after all
And what are we all but mares?
That eat, race and rest.
Why whip us?
O divine mother Goddess?
Thou *art* all powerful.

Baby blue eyes

Sex,
You,
Me,
Table light.

Closer to heaven baby,
Are we staging a fright scene?
Miles and miles away.
Moving away,
Slowly moving away.

I can't,
See,
In,
Your eyes.

You forget,
What,
It takes,
To,
Raise.
My soul.

You, crouching, climbing, descending,
Me, lassoing around you,
We move heavenwards!
With surging force.
And I contemplate death.
Death of the body, death of the heart.

(You made love to me. You chose me. Somewhere miles and miles away. I see
you. Baby blue eyes.)

On this stone,
I hit my head,
Bleed,
Dirty passion,
Relive my youth,
Safe...
Safe...
Secure...

And you curious fairy,
Damn
With blood
All those who restrain.

Jerk-off

"Don't do this,
I can't live without you",
She cried, he walked away
She ran and followed,
She didn't let him 'escape'.

"If you do this one more time,
I'm done with you",
But baby one more night,
One more hit,
And I will be done with this shit.
It ain't killing me no more,
To be dancing with this other 'lover'.

She calls, I respond
You cried,
I didn't listen,
I walked away.
But this hapless road leads nowhere
Just round and round in circles.

So I was where I was,
And you walked away.

Now something is creeping inside of me,
I don't miss you much, no.
But you hurt me, I needed that
I'm such a subdued masochist.

This ocean is so deep,
I've been trying to float without a raft.

I'm not a murderer, I'm not a rapist, I'm not a thief
Why do you hate me, why do you despise me so?
I am but lost and jaded.

This part is for you Lord,
Hope you are listening
I am trying, I am trying, Lord
I have found the light,
Now all I have to do is give up this cloak
And enter the good kingdom.

This part is for you Mom,
I know you have tried, a lot
But really it is me who has to try,
You can only give me guidance and support.
And your love.

And Dad, there is a reason I mentioned you last
I never meant to hurt you,
I am not weak,
I am just one of the unfortunate thousands
Who can't control their addictions.
Dad, you are losing hope
And I am gaining hope everyday.
Why this silly equation, this absurd chemistry?
I miss my jolly father.

I need you again in this poem, my Lord
Everything seems to be dying

Can it be revived?
Can the dead come back to life?
Not men, but love, and care and happiness?

Raunak Baral

The quill of Icarus

When men fall,
They set their hungry dogs upon them
And in the midst of blood and bone
They celebrate the conquest of their intestines.

Those who have wings shall fly
What are cages?
They will open with time.

What God does strike those down
Who have erred but as humans do,
Not caused any great infamy
But lived peaceful among men
In good humour and love.

But as legends say,
Icarus has to fall.
For he desired things beyond the reach
Of ordinary humans.
He desired to be beyond ordinary.

But little do demons know
That tore Icarus limb from limb
Devoured his flesh
And defiled his name.
That he is not an ordinary bird,
But a phoenix that rises with such rage
That in its fire it burns the enemies' hide.

Time Travelling my life(1)

King of distant lands,
Sparrows of disaster
Gelled well with my money
Talking to strangers
Laughing at disaster.
Ha Ha Ha.

You're not hardcore,
No you ain't.
You are just another part of me
So that spear you hold
Is just another poker
In the fire of your own funeral.
Maharaja, be satisfied.

I won't be laughing at your funeral
For you're going up in flames
In ashes and incense
And I'm going down,
Down in the ground...

Raunak Baral

The youngest critic

If you've ever stood up and wondered,
Why you see dark rain falling
Or maybe you have seen angels crying.
Know that great men shall still walk on this earth,
And their greatness shall pervade in your hearts.

You and your neighbour will feel each other like brothers,
When his wife will be the mother of your child, in love
And your wife the mother of his.
You will cry and look to the distance.
What if I said, look no further
This glorious task:
You have to undertake.

Yes, you, the one with the unruly, long hair
You who's afraid of public speaking
You who broke your leg while dancing,
And think you can never dance again.
And lastly, you the photographer and the poet
The eyes of society,
Play the lyres of poesy,
Or focus the sunlight in your lens
On THIS young child.

His mother hasn't returned home since last night,
There's not a morsel of bread in the house
His father lies drunk in a corner,
His cries are unheard.

God bangs his hand hard on the table,
"Wheres't thou see such dreams?"
And I answer,
In the minds of your lovers, Sir.
"Lovers?", sayeth he
Yes, the people who have faith in their heart
That one day you shall descend,
In whatever form you desire
And people of the world will call you by whatever name
From Mecca to Vatican.
And that day the world shall need me no more.
The youngest critic will have died.

Raunak Baral

The reason

It was a sunny day,
Yes it was.
You stood underneath that tree,
and you smiled at me.

I was already in love with you,
That kind of love that plays hide-and-seek.
Suddenly everything was red,
And I was transported,
Back.

I was suspended,
Floating in midair
My hands fighting to grab you
But you were, so far away.

I dreamt of you in red and white,
Sari.
Your feet painted in red,
Your smile like the moody moon,
Slightly curled.

I thought I'd never fall,
But I fell,
My legs are broke
But I'm limping
And I'll limp all the way to you
Till my life gives up.

Because you are the reason
I'm alive.

Raped me?

You couldn't mend me with your kind words,
Not with your slaps,
Not with your psychedelic drugs,
Not with political discussions,
Not with riots, coups
Not with sarcasm,
Not with force
Not with pseudo-freedom.
I'd still say my soul is free.

You called me talkative,
You called me irritating,
You called me misbehaved,
You called me a retard,
You called me mad.
But was I the only one seeing sanity in
Not sucking out the ass of other people
And their theories and their opinions.

Now you'll call me a man without ideals
And I'll tell you ideals last as long as you reach the goal,
You'll call me a man without morale,
I've fought and won more times than you.

Some people live their lives for achieving,
Others for earning money,
Still others for being happy.
I live my life for making things beautiful and easy,
And fight wrong when I see it.
I am no superhero,
I am the anti-villain.

Raunak Baral

Not a word...

On the near hill,
There was a clearing,
A valley of sorts.

And there I lie,
getting reborn from my flames.
I burn everyday, to free myself from my sins
And everyday I am reborn from the ashes.

Fire, earth, wind and soul
Strengthen my being
My existence,
My Karmic sword.

You ignorant men and women
You laugh at my plight,
Thou shall not do so
When I take flight and look down upon you.

And then like pepper balls in a jar,
You shall look to me.
Small people.
People who once envied and hated me.

Fool you are woman,
That you do not understand my true value,
I shall be great,
And you shall repent.

This is a promise,
Not a word.

Tomorrow was sure to happen

So you danced. And I watched. I held my drink in my hand. Your heels made love to the floor. Pulling with intensity, like a passionate harlot.

You danced alone. And couples surrounded you. This was the dream vacation. A second honeymoon. Passionate Latino music lulled in the background. The drops of sweat on your forehead formed with perfect precision, making you wear a glassy skull cap. Anything shiny was beautiful. Atleast in my eyes.

I took the notepad. I wrote a short note. I left it on the seat for her eyes. And I walked towards the beach.

I watched her from a distance. The light made her look little now, from this distance. She was still dancing.

I sipped my drink.

She sensed my absence. She turned around to look. I wasn't there. She was coming closer to the deck. She found the note. I saw her smiling and looking around.

Now she was making her way to the beach, walking her slutty kind of walk. Criss crossing her legs more than usual. Her breasts heaved with her every move. Her black dress shifting up and down around her thighs exposing smooth, soft skin. I grew hard watching her, in anticipation.

She crossed the foyer and was plunged in darkness. I waited for her to cross me. I hid in the darkness.

She crossed me. I grabbed her from the back. She let out a cry of shock, then burst into laughter. I started kissing her neck. She exposed her neck for me.

I didn't bother with the zip. I uncupped her breasts. They were soft, like clouds of cotton. She turned around, and in the moonlight her eyes shone like diamonds. She kissed me. It was magical.

We scrambled to get out of our clothes. The sand was soft and smooth. Whenever I stopped, or lost energy, she turned around and straddled me. It was perfect chemistry.

Then slowly she climaxed. Her mouth grew into an O, and she let out a few heavy, deep breaths, then she collapsed on me. But kept moving from beneath her waist. I came second.

Then spent, we both lay on the beach nibbling each other's bodies.

There was no talk of tomorrow, for tomorrow was sure to happen.

Absolution

Two friends met in darkness. Me and my soul. He was holding a glass in his hand. The beckoning was too hard, I drank the first sip. I felt my head reeling, and things moving out of control.

Soon we were herdsmen wearing cloaks and leading herds through grassy meadows of heaven, the sky was low, the clouds were barely above us.

There was a slightly sinister quality about the light, it was as if a great portent was about to open up infront of us.

We reached a great wall...he turned around and looked at me, faceless as he was and he told me "The drink is called Rakija, my friend"....

Wait...wasn't that the name of the song I was listening to before I lost control, and everything turned to darkness?

I sought God, as if in a casual trapped reverie where he usually reveals himself... The wall blocked everything that came in its path...

Now I was a bit anxious my friend was waiting there beside me and he wasn't saying a word...I forgot about him. I started calling names of angels, and everything I had ever read up in texts that swore to be holy.

Just then what seemed like the sun, what was providing the light came upon my head...and it hung in midair...

Out of the corner of my eyes I saw my soul turn into a *shadow*. It flew slowly towards me and became my butterfly wings...or so I thought(I don't have eyes at the back of my head).

"Father, I understand why you have put up this wall in my path..."

Silence.

"I am ready to wing..."

Silence.

"I have absolved my sins...I am a free man now"

An explosion. The ground infront of me flew up in the air, and out of that came black smoke and around me started running objects of evil and temptation.

Objects that I had left behind.

The last temptation...that's what lay beyond the wall...

"Are you ready to face your final temptation? Failing to withdraw yourself from which will give you a lifetime of misery and anguish?"

"In your glory, let me bask", I said.

And there she was! Dressed in her most seductive, she came towards me... planted a kiss on my mouth...I watched her with measured anger. Suddenly I was in hell, and the devil started playing the piano...Oh the devil's song...made me jumpy! She started dancing to the tune...and frequently she would pull me, and whisper blasphemies in my ears...

"You take God's name in vain...remember how good we are? Remember?"

And then she laughed her evil bitchy laughter, her companion pulled me by the hook again...and again I did not have the strength to fight back...and I started flying towards them like everytime...but this time my wings started flapping...I stopped midway...I took the hook out of my neck...

And would you believe it? I flew away!

I was free! Free again! I flew among the clouds...I flew next to the sun...as it flew with me...

I was flying! I was free!

But wait?! My herd? I left them behind...just then a kindly voice told me... sometimes we must leave even the most faithful behind...for they cannot travel any farther...

I turned back to see their longing expressions...as I flew away...farther and farther away...

Raunak Baral

This path that I walk

When you are floating in your altruistic dreams,
Do you notice a life that is passing by?
A dream unfulfilled
Or a place not visited?
Laughed he at me.

Who are you?
Death, he said, but call me destiny,
If you fear the name.

Don't you know?
I said.
That I'm on my own
On this road, and setting suns I do see
And I see them rising as well.
I do not question where the road is leading me.

I do not deviate,
For the path is straight.
And so many things I have seen.

Have you stopped running?
Said he?
Yes.
Said I.
From what were you running?
Society, fear, shame?
Or maybe from me?

No, said I.
I was caught in space and time,
And I started running to break that enchantment
Of Love and Maya.
Now I walk a path,
One that has been shown to me.

Death you say you are,
And meet you I will at the end of this road
But destiny, if I may call you so,
I wish to be your friend,
So that when I change my karma!
You may not begrudge me!

Time is the best healer my friend!
Even broken wings mend in time...

Raunak Baral

A strange smile

Today a drop of alcohol didn't pour down Mr. Dutta's glass,
Today the children of the house are flying kites
Today the women of the house are wearing sindoor again,
Leaving behind their jeans and shirts.

Because today is a sunny day,
Yes my friend, there are cirrus clouds in the sky
And if you had a cone, I would give you a dollop of that vanilla.
Today, I am not wearing my writer's cap!
Today, I am free from the vestiges of yesterday.

Today I refused a joint and I refused a drink
I played cricket with children and old men alike,
Today is a sunny day in Maidan.

Today I have 45 rupees in my pocket,
15 spent on the bus,
15 spent on papri chaat,
And 15 on balloons.

I gave the balloons away to street children
And I saw their face light up.
Then by an occurence of chance I fished my pockets
And I found 5 rupees,
I bought an orange lolly.

I was about to put it in my mouth
When I saw a child without a shirt on.
My parents had taught me to,
Share things with others.
So I offered the lolly to the kid.
He gave me a strange smile and disappeared.
He gave me a strange smile...

What I envision in you

You are mortal in your structure,
In your blood and flesh,
In your dreams and reveries
You are Superman
This world's saviour.

I weep a single tear for you,
Embrace what is good and what is free
Because nothing beckoned you like the robin's call,
Does not mean that you shall stop seeking,
Love and Beauty and Friendship, my friend.

Enter this world of jagged sharp images,
Old posters of you hanging from theatres of old
People raising a glass to your honour,
Under the streetlights of Paris.
Why exist as a skeleton in a grave you dig?

Find yourself today,
Where you exist in excited whispers
On the lips of a few ladies, cheeks freshly painted with vermillion
Sit down, forget the childhood obsession
Which came floating like a tuft of cloud.

Exist forever, winger, friend, keep that holy smoke coming where it comes
from. I am there to take care of you....

Love,
Raunak.

Raunak Baral

Wait for me

Ting-a-ling-ling,
That's the way my heart goes.
Shall we be friends, or shall we be foes?
The sunshine in your laughter
Or in your funny sarcasm,
Fills me with joy and hope.

If we are friends,
Then we shall build a treehouse
And play scrabble and chat all day,
With coffee!

I never hear lovers lament
This beautiful feeling called love,
How it makes its way back and back again,
In my heart.

Find your place in my heart
And I will give you a place in my dreams,
Together we're going to go for a walk in the woods,
Holding hands.

Wait for me.

I used you

So if you were to
Wake up with me beside you,
What would you do if I told you
There's a door that works only one way from here
Out, out, out.

Your teardrops they fall, dry and sultry
But leave, leave, leave I did
And memories of you pulled me back
Into satanic slavery.

If you were to rape your own emotions
Be real gangsta,
Don't let the thunder fall upon me.
Do you want, do you want, did you want
To die? Really, really, really?

Believe me I stopped loving you the day
I walked away,
But there was a little part of me that still wanted to be with you
But I felt no guilt in making love
To other women.

Add a spike to this wheel
Fire and ice, the earth will reel
If I told you my feelings for you were real,
Because I cheated on you while you were still there.

Now there's a stumbling block that I crossed
And I'm a much stronger man now
Women look at me with respect
Not a boy anymore, you see
Gravity, gravity.

You do remember how you were amazed by me
Flattered much I felt at your words,
Now noone flatters me and that's the way I like it,
Men shouldn't be subject to flattery
It is a device we keep for women to secretively
Guide our way in through their invulnerable shells.

You treated me like a boy, ladyo
Life treats me like a man.
I got problems, real problems
Bigger than you can handle,
Your phoney little arse.

Now if I were to complete this poem you would know...
And I don't intend on giving that to you...
Like once I told you, before
I used you...
And you thought this was love.
I am sorry.
I have mended my ways, and I felt the first apology should go to you.

Blemishes

Frequency in my ear,
Everyone staring at me
Why do they stare?
Can't they see
Just how hard, I'm trying.

Wheels of karma turning and turning
And I was asked to pull the weight
I am repenting for my sins
Won't you take this load off me?

There's going to be a royal jury,
People walk towards the court
Public jury, red nosed Indian gentlemen
Here to see the trial of the innocent.
Move these shackles off me
The fires of hell are too hot.

Society stands and boos
The juvenile delinquent brought to justice
Such a scandal society just couldn't resist.
Right from when they brought him back home
And then they took him again, in binds.

There's a huge black mark on my face doctor,
Does plastic surgery help?

Raunak Baral

The way I'd like you to be

So I was space trippin'
Looking for so much love,
There was so much space
And I could hear my own voice.

Looking for somebody to release my woes,
So these spacy creatures come bouncing
They start a' dancing,
We started singing
We were shooting so fast in the cosmos.

I can't get some action with all that sex-u-ality
All it takes is some meditation
About what she likes or not
And whether I give it my all
Depends really, on her mood.

Some people can't stand their own reflections,
My reflection is my own favourite enemy
The more it resists
The stronger I grow,
Till it bows down
And does my hair the right way.

Baby I could hold your waist in my arms
And make you believe
There is a man inside us all,
But be my bitch tonight.

Let us not talk about money
'Cause I have none
But I could set your soul on fire
With senseless talks of freedom,
Holding hands while walking down an aisle
At a mall.

I want your body,
Your face and your eyes
Don't mistake me
For lies I give you none
I will worship you till the end of time.

Nature's bounty

Grudgingly walking away
From his last drink,
Woman swooned
Gin and lime consumed
Kingdoms conquered,
Penis and Vagina,
The words were on every mute mannequin's lips
In the bar.

Conjured up in unholy pentagons,
Demons assisted
Lighting candles and blowing holy smoke
Into his nostrils.
The smell of sweat was driven away
By expensive perfume.

On stone carved stairs,
Lay prostitutes of Old
Their flexible bodies and outstretched legs inviting.

The devil in his mind he penetrated,
Gin and lime started talking
"Redemption!", screamed his other face.
Moved in and out,
Moved in and out.

Sailors were braving the lightning,
Tumultuous ocean, traitor onboard
Secret of the ship unfolded
Victory of the day went to the youth,
Who in his dreams was walking the board.

Splash! He was drowning,
Swallowed whole by a whale
He was now a miner in a stomach
Plucking weed, and cleaning, always cleaning.

Then suddenly,
The sun rose, as Ra poured cauldrons of oil on everyone's body
Each bloody vampire burnt in the brightness of the rising sun.
Their bodies aflame,
Saintly men prayed for their souls on the ghats of Benares,
As they thronged naked and wearing spectacles to see the smoke rising.

Suddenly he was moving heavenward,
But the sky was an illusion
Love of nature was a lie,
His wings were clipped, and as the smoke moved heavenward
He came down like rain upon all things.
His love, his hatred the creator of all things
The mover and shaker,
Salt and pepper,
Dead love letters.

Then came the curse,
Inscribed in time, by flaming golden verses
Licking his beard
It burnt his face
Ugliness!
Women irked, children bothered
They laughed,
At his ugliness.
Nature's love bountiful
A prince to a pauper,
A knight to a grotesque.

Moving, moving
His words inconsequential
Trampled on by weaker men,
His limbs tied
His oratory gone, tongue tied to the mouth
Worms eating his reason.

Heaven eludes him,
Hell has him
Pain suspends him
Shame writes him
Love discards him.
What do you call such a man?

Anarchy Theory

Burn the bed you're sleeping on,
'Cuz there's no mothers telling fairytales.
It's just a dystopic world, selling vinyl dreams.
Dreaming is banned, don't aspire too high,
Fall you will, into a pit of worms
Which will feed off your skin.

Reality is just an illusion,
A treatment of childish stories,
Which we've learnt to see, hear and like.
Millions die, millions starve,
Millions crave to see the faces of their mothers and fathers.
But we shot down all the stars!

I close my eyes, and I see little soldiers in Tianenmen dreaming,
Getting crushed by highrises,
Their graves covered by sand and cement.
I see Syrian mothers carrying babies out of hell,
Their faces contorted with the pain of passion.

Such little babies toll the deep dark knell,
Dying sounds abound.
Holy mercedeses stop at the sight of black cats crossing.
God wakes up in his nightmare.
Our churches, our pagodas, the cost of his sins.

In this darkness called life there seems to be
Only one light at the end of this tunnel,
That too being sold at the cost of our souls,
Weighing against gold and silver.

The Buddhist soldier burns in the flames of sin,
The sin of another man
The atrocities of imperialism, stop like a cork
Emotions coming straight out of the heart.

Every life measured by the ounce they earn in the day,
The richest man has three convertibles,
Two wives,
And an army of sluts, guards, and soldiers.

Insanity was the answer,
Insanity was the saviour,
Insanity was the curer,
Insanity was wiser.

No more pain...

Walking on the sidewalk,
making some trouble
making some trouble,
Yeah I'd be making some trouble.

Sniffing glue day and night
Sliding on a slippery highway,
Branches of a day's antiquity
Mixing in the setting sun.

Black tentacles of the devil inside
Gripping me vice like,
All hope lost,
The day comes to an end.

Before another one starts
The power steps down from the cosmos
And frees my soul from its shackles
Every night,
Every night I am free.

Hitting rock bottom,
Slipping up again
Common misfortune.

I found faith the day our Lord
Came back from the heavens
And unburdened my soul
Of all grief
This is what I dream.
This is what I fight for.

No more pain.
No more pain.

Seasons...

The summer slowly faded to winter, the wet mud tracks slowly hardened and got covered by grass, it is yellow now. We met everyday, you lied to your father and met me by the lake. You would let me keep my head on your lap and you would read me a story. Time, fate, destiny were immaterial. Utopia of such sort, I had not found before.

I once asked you to wear a Sari, and you wore one for me, green and blue it was, swirling, twirling, your peacock paradise. I noticed that, from being a virgin girl, you had turned into a sweeping woman with radiance in your face and your eyes. As time passed, you grew up from your papa's lap and dungarees and short skirts to saris and salwars. I wanted to paint your forehead with vermillion. It fit well with the 'rasa' of your demeanour.

Summer was too short, and winter was too long, you would cover me in the gentle fabric of your pashmina. Krishna and his sakhis played in the gardens while you played with my hair.

I always wondered where did the story end. In summer, in winter? I could not touch a season. Spring painted my face with colours, and you disappeared in your myriad hues.

Radhe

Twirling in the December breeze
A maple leaf touched
A teardrop,
Carefully preserved in an ocean.
A djinn glided from its element
To this place
Of fake smiles
And melting plastic masks.
Among demons was beset
Me, I picked myself up
From the treasure chambers of
Ancient Emperors.
I hear you say,
I heard you say
My name.
Do you still say?
Stay!
For just when the ice is melting
Like a porcelain jug in a pool of hot milk
Floating in it are pure white swans
Of such brilliance as the tears in your eyes.
If I were a honeycomb
I would catch your tears, and keep them in my midst.
I would be like the long winding mountain road
Carelessly entwining around your breast.
Love me, like a child
Be one again
Like when I found you
My Radhe, my Radhe.

Raunak Baral

Is it getting any better?

Since I was young
I have heard, seen and felt
Blood.

Gushing out of my privates,
Or slowly trickling down
From the mouth of men
After drunken fights.

In this dark room with the red light for company
The tears my mother has cried
Seems like blood too.

Winter, like a demoness
Plays her sad violin
As he moves in and out of me
Pinning me down.

I am hollow
I am a scarecrow,
I move among lights
And do the darkness' bidding.

I am a solitary figure
Do not call me a name
For I am afraid of the weight that
I would have to carry.

I pain, I pain for you
For I know my pain would appease you.
Tonight, I will cry for you,
I will bleed for you,
I will sell my soul for you.

You who violated my sanctity
I will pray so that you do it again.
Murder my mind
You know I can't believe you
But still I can't leave you,
I will cry, cry for you.

I will take my kohl
I will paint a door on this wall
And you can come in.

I will lovingly tie you to my bed
Make love to you one last time
And you will feel my blood on your lips
And there,
Underneath the ashen sky
I will die in your arms.

Raunak Baral

Blue Olivia

Blue torn rags of firefly cloak,
Floated in the abissynthian walls of my mind,
Fires burnt as oracles spoke,
Hands of fire breathed ashen scripts down my naked spine;
Rudiments of my broken heart died in your dead space.

Death Wish

The darkest days sometime start with a glorious morning,
I watched the sun rise from Ra's arm in Hamunaputra.
I was standing infront of a lake
The black water reflected the curled fangs of the sun in the murk,
With my finger I sent an angry ripple towards it,
And looked around me,
Locked up,
Lonely,
Solitary,
Hurt,
Murderous.
Numb,
Humiliated.

I felt like Jesus on the cross,
as faces floated around me
laughing at my hurt,my bleeding limbs
my weak limbs, my failing limbs.

My head hurt from last night's torture,
My stomach ached from hunger
And my shoulders drooped from overwork
My eyes were diamondlike from the cold and the wind.

If this weren't the end then I didn't know what was,
I have lost everything,
I had given half of it away long back in a bequest of the heart
And now half of it lies torn and tattered.

I am a dead man,writing a dead song.

Raunak Baral

The augery of David and Claire

Listen to the rain outside
Like birds without wings they fall
On paper it seems
I turned to the night outside the small window
Of the room,
And contemplated the augery outside.
Fragile rainclouds filled the night sky,
Blushing pink like an unwilling bride,
Is it why they cry?
Is it why the night seems so dark?
For in starry nights, I have seen
Blackness engulfing me,
But never have I felt lightless, lifeless, loveless.
It is this crying night sky
That sometimes makes me wonder
My love, shall we ever meet?
The stranded smiles of the night sky
Still elude me, and I still look for the answer.
I ask the universe,
You brought the crying hearts of two
Dark clouds together,
And though a despondent couple they do make,
A couple still be it.
I ask the Great Divide,
God, You left man's hand one day
But wasn't there the promise of protection
Of love, of care?
What about two bleeding hearts
Seeking each other in a valley
Full of people, where Jesus stands, his heart
wide open and we run to him,
and he gives us names
I am called David and you Claire.
Jesus was there.

Where were you God?
Where are you Claire?
We met in dreams,
And through magic windows,
Together we wielded that magic wand
That bound our souls to an eternal, undying love.
I stopped. I said, "I do"
And you?
What would you say if we met on such a rainy night,
And if just I was carrying an umbrella?
And you were getting wet, so I said,
"If you don't mind, then we can stand together"
Would you stand with me, like you would
Stand on our wedding dais,
Preparing to take me as yours and yours only
Say, "I do", Claire
And I will take you away to my magical kingdom
Which now misses a Queen.
And Jesus will be there blessing our path
And I will say unto him,
"I am not worthy to be called thy son,
But I have returned,
And I am willing to serve as thy hired hand
As thou will show me."

Raunak Baral

Love game

I watched amazed
As pixies played, with
Your hair blowing wild in the wind
Like a yellow lily
You frowned upon my heart
Stalling a love game
That we never played.
Love game; that sweet love game.

The space rollercoaster

Slide in gently gentlemen,
And take your seats.
And after you are done with removing all metal items
Just press the button.

Well my name is Bouzouzou,
And tonight gentlemen
As you are aware,
We shall be starting a new era in space travel.

Questions? Before I start getting weary and stop talking?
Yes sir, you over there,
What? Yes you're damn right we're going on this space rollercoaster
No sir, nothing fancy like space planes.
Yes sir, you'd very well want to hold on to your top hat.

Engage.

So they rolled, funny, like ducks in a row, up and down
Like cha-cha,
Chug Chug, they went up in the sky
Like a long wiggly snake against the moon.
And the wind was so strong in their faces
That they looked like flattened dough flying in air.

You should know that there are no pink elephants in space
Because they are so heavy that they cannot float in air
And pink elephants do not exist.

Gentlemen, on your left, The Moon!
And everybody cheered and clapped.
Up, up and up they went,
And some hats flew down
Twirling and twirling like leaves falling.

Okay gentlemen, now we shall be facing the lack of gravity
And by now everyone was drunk with the champagne in their boxes,
So everyone laughed and cheered and clapped.
So the first person flew out into space from his seat,
Hey! Look at that! A flying man in outer space! How strange!
They'll be writing about this in The Time for ages.
And everyone pointed and laughed.
The flying man laughed too, and waved back.

And then some others flew out of their seats,
And went vaulting into space.
And since without gravity you can't stay still in one place
They looked like they were dancing in space,
Going circle, or rotating.
And they weren't sumo wrestlers,
Because that would have looked funnier.

Cheerio, gentlemen! Space dancers!
Now who wants to join them?
And because everybody was drunk,
A lot of people raised their hands.
So if you will just ease yourselves out of your seats, and there you go!
So everyone was space dancing.
And it looked like magic,
Against the crescent moon.
Now if the crescent moon had smiled,
Then it would have been crossing limits.
But in dreams one can never have enough.

So, I woke with a dreary eye
My ears ringing with the voices of happy space dancers
And I realised,
How this poem lacks rhyme or meter
Which made me sad,
Because in most poems there is rhyme and meter
Which is okay,
And I thought rhyme and meter is overrated.
So maybe another day.

Mom

Goodnight Mom, you're so far away
Not here to wish me night
No lullabies, no bedtime stories,
You're not here to ruffle my hair,
And rock me to sleep.

Goodnight mom, I look at the stars above
They put me to sleep
And sing me songs.
You held my hand as I walked
over rock and vale,
As I grew up and when I fell.

You raised me up like a rock in the middle of the sea
Wearing all storms, fighting it out,
You raised me up to more than I could be.

I held your hand through fire and through rain
You told me stories and kept me calm
Till there was sunshine again.
You took care of us in the bad times and the good
You knew exactly what I needed
Exactly what to cook.

Goodnight mom, I hope you are safe
I miss you a lot.
I hope you get a good night's sleep
As the angels fly above
And pour heavenly sands of sleep
Upon your closing eyes.
Goodnight mom, sweet dreams till sunrise.

All night long

It's four in the morning,
And we are dancing, the night away
Your head on my shoulders
And my hand around your waist.

You are still smelling of that sweet perfume
that you put, who knew I could
Feel so good, with you right here.

I want to feel your tenderness all night long,
Spend all night with you, dance to this sweet song
I wish the day never breaks
Let us go wherever our feet take us
Let love consume us.

We'll dance all night long,
To this sweet little song
Sugar honey, when you look at me and smile
And we move a step or two
Time stands still, and my love explodes
We'll take a hundred different roads
We'll walk a hundred paths
To ease the pain of our tender hearts.

Take my hands honey
Let's dance all night long
To our favourite song
This moon is never going to set
A lovelier woman I have never met
And with you, I shall dance
All night long.

Raunak Baral

The Telephone is Ringing

The telephone is ringing,
And I am wondering
Who it could be?
For she doesn't call at this time.
I am alone in my peaceful abode,
That I put blood and sweat to build.

The telephone is ringing,
I am wondering whether I should pick it up,
Maybe it's my boss or a colleague of mine.

I am musing ten years hence,
And ten years is enough for bringing reckoning day.
The familiar sights that we see today,
Maybe they won't cross the line.
The people we love will be dead and gone,
We just pray and wish in the air we breathe
That everyone crosses the line.

The telephone is ringing,
And the familiar ring-ring haunts me
When it used to bother me ten years back, obviously this day
For I am imagining ten years hence.
When my father's phone used to ring on Sundays,
Disturbing family time,
And my father used to get engrossed in the telephonic conversation,
And the smile on his face seemed so natural
More natural than the inscrutable expression he had,
When he was listening to me.

It is ten years hence,
And I have bought my way out of that familiar ring-ring
Peace finally fills my home.
We'll be lunching on the greens today,
Everyone, including me,
And there will be some children lolling in the background.

The telephone is ringing,
It is saying
One day we all grow old,
And we think about the stories we could have told.

Raunak Baral

A Prayer

Caught in between,
I sail on the tide
Which moves me from shore to shore.
I gurgle water sometimes,
As I try to stay afloat.

Fate cuts me a mean line,
One that I have to walk,
It hurts to see others are walking
In boulevards.
While I'm walking on a miserable line.

I see hands coming at me,
"Come, I'll see you through..."
They say.
But me, I'm happy in this parched land
That situations have lent me.
I just want to get a day's peace.

I didn't do the right things at
The right time.
That's why so much suffering surrounds me.
I know many others like me,
They are not living like me,
They have two square meter ground beneath them.
And I have none.

So if you go away from my life right now,
I will fall again.
Into that deep abyss,
And noone shall care,
Noone shall pick me up.
Let me be, Oh good Lord,
Your glory is all I seek
Let me be the person I am.
My wants are not many.

Pretty Pur

She stood, a gorgeous diva
Holding some vegetable leaf in her hand
And calm, smooth eyes like hot coal
Threatening the storekeeper,
As if saying, "Trust me, you don't know how much this leaf costs!
It takes a man to know…"
And the storekeeper just dismisses it with his hands,
To much dismay of his "man" hood
Then she walked out of the store,
Prancy like a pixie fairy in 60s clothes.
She put her 60s shades on
And oh oh oh, the laserbeam destroyed half the street.
Ladies and Gentlemen, presenting to you, "Pretty Pur".
God made her, after raving in Goa, falling in love in the forests
Getting drunk on the beach, and waking up in a hippie camp,
Later getting a tattoo on his arm saying "Mighty Me".
Then to spoil all the fun Pegasus landed in the middle of the fanfare
While he was juggling electricity to show off, and carried him off
Back to his lonely abode in Olympus.
So he vowed to make someone who would embody the amazing party he had,
Back on planet Earth.
Way back on planet Earth.

So he brought his Godly tools,
Human limbs, and eyes and brains
Caviar and cigarettes and wine, but that was only for him.
Limb by limb he made her perfect, and called her by a name only He could call
"Pretty Pur!"
And he laughed his mountainous laughter, and the sky thundered
Lightning fell.
Pretty pur mewed out of God's cauldron and straight into his arms.
God held her tight and tried to put a leash around her neck,
Oh how sweet they would seem when they both would go out for a walk
In Arcadia.

Pretty Pur shrieked when she saw the leash, God's china plates fell and broke
Then she snaked and swirled around God's body and ferreted out of notice.
Now God started crying,
He would never go to Goa again.
Poor Him!

Raunak Baral

Love makes you leap

I haven't seen you for months,
But I am hopeful, somehow you'll show up
Maybe we'll meet over a teacup,
Or at a party.

And this time I'll ask you to dance,
And you'll say you really don't know how to,
So I'll just stand there make polite conversation,
Love is the same here as in every other nation.

I'll tell you how beautiful you are,
And how lost you are
In this sea of admirers,
In your eyes the beauty of yore.

I love you like the sea loves the beach,
I love you like birds love the wind,
You touched my soul and you made me sink.
Yeah you made me sink.

Doesn't matter if you're in a dress
Or a Kimono.
I'd look into your eyes,
And if I feel love,
I'll hold your hand.
But if I still see surprise like I saw last time,
Then I will take your stupid test,
Which you know best.

I love you like the sea loves the beach,
I love you like birds love the wind,
You touched my soul and you made me sink.
Yeah you made me sink.

The Reason

It was a sunny day,
Yes it was.
You stood underneath that tree,
and you smiled at me.

I was already in love with you,
That kind of love that plays hide-and-seek.
Suddenly everything was red,
And I was transported,
Back.

I was suspended,
Floating in midair
My hands fighting to grab you
But you were, so far away.

I dreamt of you in red and white,
Sari.
Your feet painted in red,
Your smile like the moody moon,
Slightly curled.

I thought I'd never fall,
But I fell,
My legs are broke
But I'm limping
And I'll limp all the way to you
Till my life gives up.

Because you are the reason
I'm alive.

Raunak Baral

The phoenix . . . restored

Everything in shambles,
The phoenix lay in ashes
And hot ember.
His enemies he could not remember.
Was it him or maybe her?
Well that doesn't matter now,
All that does is evolution.
Slowly the ashes will turn to muscles and veins,
Blood will flow,
The sparkle in his eyes restored,
He will fly,
But for now penance for his bloodied soul.
He suffers and he suffers still,
For evil deeds and acts unknown,
For when his dearly beloved forgive him,
He will once again be whole.

Our friday cup of tea

She undressed,
She threw her hair open
Like the black tempest.
She said she just wanted to be a woman,
I licked her toes
Sending shivers up her body.

Then I gave her enough reason to be a woman,
I embraced her
And she accepted me, wholly.

Holy or pagan worship,
We were bonding like rain at the edge of lightning,
Murdering the sacred 'rose'
Her voice hit a high note at staccato.

Like double deckers crashing into each other,
Glass flying everywhere,
There wasn't a piece of you I left untouched.

Love in alchemist's tongue is
Transformation of the heart
Into a metal of the purest quality
Such lustre, is rarely seen.

It was raining
And I had waited for you behind my window,
Tree for company
I have whiled away the hours
Time for your visit,
Our evening cup of tea
Every Friday.